Marks on Paper

Essays on drawing, seeing and looking

by Suzanne Visser

April 2023

Image on cover: Suzanne Visser

ISBN eBook: 978-0-6457074-3-4

ISBN Print: 978-0-6457074-2-7

Clear Mind Press, Australia

Copyright © Suzanne Visser

Legal deposit in the National Library of Australia

Design and layout: Clear Mind Press

www.clearmindpress.com

Typesetting: Clear Mind Press - Baskerville 12

Cover Design: Clear Mind Press

Marks on Paper

Essays on drawing, seeing and looking

Suzanne Visser

Table of Contents

About the book   10
About the author 12
From the brain to the hand 15
Perspective and colour 29
What do marks on paper do to us? 32
Life Drawing 36
Chris Tate 39
Looking and seeing 43
Looking, a short but rather precise observation 50
It takes two to tango, always two 53
Marks draw us 55
Dynamic drawing - An ode to Ron Curran 58
How not to write about art 62
Seeing 67
Taking credit 74
The role of money, power and sex and the cult of
personality in the arts 79
Looking here, looking there 83
When the artist and the viewer disappear 88
Where painting and language meet - Ode to Japan 90
Movement 94
Paper 97
Time management 101
Ink 103

About the book

In "Marks on Paper", Suzanne Visser presents a collection of short essays that delve into the intricacies of drawing, seeing, and looking. Through her philosophical lens, Visser challenges readers to question their assumptions about perception and reality.

Drawing on her years of experience as an artist and writer, Visser offers a sharp and deep exploration of the creative process, inviting readers to consider the act of drawing as a powerful tool for self-discovery. With insights that are both poetic and practical, she examines the role of attention, intention, and intuition in the artistic process.

At its heart, "Marks on Paper" is a meditation on the human experience of perception, and a call to embrace the richness, complexity and strangeness of our visual world. With its thought-provoking essays, this book is a must-read for anyone interested in the arts, philosophy, or simply the art of seeing.

About the author

Suzanne Visser, a legal scholar, is an accomplished Australian writer, known for her works of fiction and non-fiction. She has authored an ever growing body of works, covering a diverse range of topics. Her bestselling thriller, *The Fish Murders*, has been translated into four languages, gaining widespread recognition for its gripping plot and vivid characters.

Visser's independent research work of crime in rural Australia in *The Elephant's Tooth* is widely regarded for its high academic quality, contributing significantly to the field.

Visser has been recognized for her exceptional writing skills in several languages and her ability to combine a sharp intellect with a deep understanding of human psychology.

Residing and working in Alice Springs, Visser continues to explore new areas of writing and research. Her works are known for their philosophical insights and the profound depth of their explorations. Readers can learn more about Suzanne Visser's works and research by visiting the publisher's website at:
www.clearmindpress.com
and her own website:
sustainablejusticeaustralia.com

From the brain to the hand
DRAWING

We are proud of our children's first drawings. We stick them onto the fridge with magnets. Or we even frame them and hang them on the wall for everyone to admire.

Yet they are not so different from any other child's drawings.

Two-year-olds scribble from left to right and back, adding a twirl here and there to represent a signature.

Three-year-olds are fond of circles, presumably depicting the faces of people around them. Eyes, ears and mouths land somewhere on or around the faces, all over the paper. There is fire, and there are dolphins, depending on the child's mind at the moment of drawing.

When they are aged four, children begin to connect the elements. The sun goes in the sky, the house on the ground, the tree next to the house, the basket in Mum's hand.

The connection between the brain and the hand is still wide open. The marks on the paper are fresh. That's why they appeal to us so much.

The child focuses on the process of drawing, not on the result.

This changes at around the age the child goes to

primary school. At the age of five or six, children begin imitating other pictures. They draw what they think they should draw according to their environment, their peers, and what they see at school and in books. and other media. This stage marks the end of good drawing and the beginning of kitsch: the freshness of the marks on the paper disappears.

During the remainder of their of childhood, children draw what they learn to draw. The open, crystal-clear connection between the brain and the hand has been broken.

Very few people are aware of this. Most stop drawing when their childhood ends. Few keep drawing. Few begin drawing again during adulthood. Even fewer regain the ability to produce the freshness of line and mark-making they once had.

Most adult amateur drawers keep producing kitsch. The focus is on the result, not on the process.

A tiny fraction of humanity focuses on the process, the lines, the marks, and their quality. These are the real artists.

When a child continues to draw, they will learn things about proper drawing; most of all, the rules of perspective and foreshortening. The theory of colour is next. Then comes the use of different media and materials. When all this has been mastered, a proper drawing or painting may be the result.

What cannot be learned is talent.

A talented artist must and will unlearn all that was learned, and start again, from scratch. Everything that has been learned is still there – in the background – but this is not what the artist relies upon. This is the point at which great art can begin to emerge.

Some artists chose to go back to the very beginning: they open the gateway between their hand and brain and let nothing they have ever learned interfere. The giant scribbles of Cy Twombly come to mind.

Others make a conscious decision not to learn or know anything. They are interested in the childhood experience and rekindle it. Once they have found it, they remain in the 'child phase' and consciously shut themselves off from any other influences. Chris Tate comes to mind. There's an essay about him elsewhere in this book.

Yet others are aware of the freshness of the child's lines and blotches, the marks on paper or canvas, *and* apply the full range of knowledge they have gained. Rembrandt is one example of this kind of painter; another is Frans Hals. In their time, it was not done to deviate from the path of technical knowledge. Their response was to set aside all they had learned, reacquire the perspectives of childhood, and then retrieve the skills they had set aside. This gave them the ability to work freely within the constraints of technical knowledge that were de rigour at the time. Their lines and blotches are fresh. They are the greatest masters of all.

Cubism and other abstract movements put an end to the tradition of the master painter. Picasso is an obvious example. The comedian and art historian Hanna Gatsby calls Picasso "Pick Asshole". I think I know why. I think of it every time I say or write: "Picasso", and then I laugh.

Painters like Karel Apple and Willem De Kooning recognised the importance of the childlike, the naïve, and the primitive in painting. They emphasise the expressiveness of these styles. They incorporate these in their work to point out the restrictions of technique and learning.

What is true of drawing and paintings is true of every art form: technique alone is not enough. There must also be talent and the willingness to abandon what one has learned.

Kitsch can easily be recognised. Kitsch is drawing what you *think* you see and not drawing what you *actually* see.

Let's take an eye as an example.

Someone who produces kitsch will probably begin a drawing of a figure by drawing the eyes. They have learned that eyes are conventionally drawn in a certain way, starting with the eyelids. Then a circle is drawn between the eye lids, representing the iris. Into the circle goes a black dot. And then, oh God, no, the *eyelashes*. What they do not realise is that they most probably *cannot see* the eyes of the figure they are drawing – let alone the details of the eyes, and let alone the eyelashes. They are not looking; They are "knowing". This makes for a dreadful drawing. And even the "knowing" is not right. The main part of the eye is a ball, the eyeball, which is partly covered by two flaps of skin, the eyelids. The ball is embedded in a hole, the socket, from which it protrudes. All in all, it is a complicated landscape of concave and convex shapes that cannot be taken in at a glance at the beginning of a drawing, when the hand and brain are still inpatient.

Starting a figure with the eyes has other drawbacks. Attention might be better given to getting the overall figure onto the page first. What are the dimensions of the body parts? At what angle are they being presented? The imaginary line on which the eyes are located can be indicated at this stage; but not the eyes themselves. They come last, if at all.

Good drawers draw *what is not there*. By drawing what is not there – for example, the space around a figure, or the space between an arm and the torso – the figure emerges on the paper by itself, so to speak.

Cézanne threw a sheet over his still life after he had contemplated it for a couple of hours. He then began by painting from memory the empty spaces between the objects. The objects naturally emerged from the empty space.

Michelangelo said that David was already present

in the block of marble; his task was simply to *set him free*.

What these great artists have in common is their humility. For them, the artwork was already there, and they merely uncovered it. They did not *dis*cover; they *un*covered.

Good drawers have no need to constantly impose a sense of control. They may have a vague plan for their drawing, but they can abandon it once the hand-brain connection takes over. Lines and blotches appear, and the drawer feels that they are not the one who draws. The drawing draws itself. The drawer reveals something that *is already* there. The drawer is not *dis*covering something but *un*covering it.

Decisions made by the drawer come into conscious awareness *after* they have been made. Science has shown this repeatedly since the 1980s, when Benjamin Libet demonstrated it for the first time in his famous button-pushing experiment.

A good artist knows this instinctively. They do not take credit for the drawing.

"The drawing drew itself," they say, or: "God drew it through me" or "my hands drew it."

The drawer of kitsch, on the other hand, has a plan and sticks to it. After the eyes have been put down on paper, other body parts are added one by one, in a laborious process towards the imagined end. The end result is constantly borne in mind. A dreadful drawing has been brought into existence. Every line of the drawing is dead, and the entirety is rounded off by the addition of a huge signature. Pity the poor soul who receives it as a gift!

A good drawing or painting is never finished. The drawer decides to stop drawing, or rather, the drawing decides when the time has come to stop. The drawing or painting is still "open" to changes and remains that way.

A kitsch drawing is finished. Very, very finished.

The background in a drawing is as important as the subject of the drawing. A good drawer knows this and pays as much attention to it as to any other part of the drawing.

A drawer of kitsch treats the background as an afterthought by shading and hatching.

The drawer of kitsch always goes too far and leaves nothing to be explored. The drawing becomes unbearably dense. Mindless shading surrounds the subject matter. A monster is created. The drawer of kitsch is proud. They think they have made all the decisions. It all fits together: the blindness to reality, the shading, the huge signature, the pride, the awfulness of the drawing.

There should be a law or commandment: "Thou shalt not produce kitsch."

Let us now see whether the same is true of writing. I will copy the observations made above and substitute "writing" for "drawing". Obviously, a few other little adjustments will need to be made.

From the brain to the hand
WRITING

We are proud of the first stories our children tell us. We write them down, or even publish them for all to admire.

Yet they are not so different from other children's stories.

Words merely circulate. There is a limited pool of them in each language. They are not ours. We just rearrange them to express ourselves. Some are better at rearranging words than others. This is called talent.

The two-year-old tells incoherent stories. Her mind jumps. Her hands move....

The three-year-old is fond of telling stories about people and things around them: Mum and Dad, fire, dolphins and dinosaurs, depending on what is in the child's mind when it is telling the story.

At about the age of four, children begin to connect the elements. The sun goes in the sky, the house sits on the ground, the tree is next to the house, the basket is in Mum's hand, the dolphin lives in water and the dinosaur eats everything.

The connection between the brain and the hand is still wide open. The words in the story are fresh. That's why they appeal to us.

The child focuses on the *process* of telling a story, not on the result. This changes at around the age the child goes to primary school. At the age of five or six, children begin imitating other stories. They tell stories they pick up from their environment, their peers, and what they see at school and read in books. This is the end of good storytelling and the beginning of kitsch. The freshness of the words in the story disappears.

During the rest of childhood, children relate stories in ways they learn from other people. The open, crystal-clear connection between the brain and the mouth is broken.

Very few people are aware of this. Most stop telling stories when childhood ends. Few keep telling stories. Few begin telling or writing stories again during adulthood. Even fewer regain the ability to produce words with the freshness they once had.

Most adult amateur writers produce kitsch. The focus is on the result, not on the process.

A tiny fraction of humanity focuses on the process, the words, the paragraphs, and their quality. These are the real artists. Words just appear, just like thoughts. Nobody has any idea how. I have no idea what my next sentence is going to be when I write this.

When a child continues to tell stories, she or he will learn things about proper writing, most of all, the rules of spelling and grammar…and if they are taught well, the child will learn that these are not random but have a relationship to meaning. Literature is next. Then the use of different styles of writing. A proper story or book may result when all this has been mastered.

What cannot be learned is talent. Talent is either there, or it is not.

Some make a conscious decision not to learn or know anything. They are interested in the childhood experience and rekindle it. Once they have found it, they remain in the childlike phase and knowingly close themselves off from any influences. These are the writers who write children's books as if they are written by children, or artists like Laurie Anderson and Yoko Ono.

Magical Realism and other abstract movements put an end to the tradition of the master writer.

Children's authors recognise the importance of the child, the naïve, and the primitive. They emphasise the expressiveness of these styles. They incorporate these in their work to point out the restrictions of technique and learning.

What is true of writing is true of every art form: technique alone is not enough. There must also be talent and the willingness to abandon what one has learned. Sticking to the rules of grammar and spelling does not make literature.

Kitsch can easily be recognised even before it is

made. Kitsch is writing about what you *think* you see and not writing about what you *actually* see.

Let's take an eye as an example.

Someone who produces kitsch will probably begin describing a character by describing the eyes. She has learned that eyes are described in a certain way. First, the colour. Then the mood. Then, oh God, no, the story the eyes tell. What she does not realise is that she most probably *cannot see* the eyes of the figure she is describing, let alone the details of the eyes, let alone the colour. She is not looking; she is "knowing". This makes for a dreadful description. And even the "knowing" is not right. The main part of the eye is a ball, the eyeball, which is partly covered by two flaps of skin, the eyelids. The ball is embedded in a hole, the socket, from which it protrudes. All in all, it is a complicated landscape of concave and convex shapes that cannot be taken in at a glance at the beginning of a story (description?), when the hand and brain are raring to go

Starting to describe a character by describing the eyes has other drawbacks. Attention might be better given to getting the whole character onto the page first. What are the dimensions of the body parts? At what angle do they present themselves? The direction of the imaginary line the eyes are located on can be indicated at this stage. But not the eyes themselves. The eyes come last, if at all.

Was it Cezanne who threw a sheet over his still life after he had contemplated it for a couple of hours? He then began by painting from memory the empty spaces between the objects. The objects naturally emerged from the empty space.

Was it Michelangelo who said that David was already present in the block of marble: his task was simply to *set him free*?

Was it Suzanne Visser who said that stories are already there; they just need to be uncovered?

What these artists have in common is their humility. For them, the artwork was already there, and they merely uncovered it. They did not *dis*cover: they *un*covered.

The worse the book, the showier its cover. The obscure name of the writer screams at us: Belinda Castle. *Who the F is Belinda Castle?* John Grisham is a writer like this.

Good writers have no need to impose control from the outset.

They may have a vague plan for their story, but they can abandon it once the hand-brain connection takes over. Words and sentences appear, and the writer feels that she is not the one who is writing. The story tells itself. The writer reveals something that *is already* there. The writer is not discovering something but *un*covering it. Robert Saltzman comes to mind.

Decisions made by the writer come into conscious awareness *after* they have been made. Science has shown this repeatedly since the 1980s, when Benjamin Libet demonstrated it for the first time in his button-pushing experiment. A good artist knows this instinctively. He or she does not take credit for the story. "The story wrote itself," he says, or: "God wrote it through me."

The writer of kitsch, on the other hand, has a plan and sticks to it. After the eyes have been described, other body parts are added in a laborious process towards the imagined end. The end result is constantly borne in mind. A dreadful story is brought into existence. Its words and sentences are dead. A loud cover rounds it all off. Pity the poor soul who receives it as a gift!

A good story or book is never finished. The writer decides to stop writing, or rather, the story decides when the time has come to stop. The story is still "open" to changes and remains that way.

A kitsch story is finished. Very, very finished.

The background in a story is as important as the subject of the story. A good writer knows this and pays as much attention to it as to any other part of the story. The characters don't only have a front, but also a back. Some have a tail.

A writer of kitsch treats the background as an afterthought. Her characters are flat, like cardboard cut-outs.

A writer of kitsch uses clichés.

The writer of kitsch always goes too far in editing and leaves nothing unsaid. The story becomes unbearably dense. A monster is created. The writer of kitsch is proud. She or he thinks all the decisions have been made. It all fits together: the blindness to reality, the shading, the cardboard characters, the clichés, the loud cover, the pride, and the awfulness of the language. There should be a law or commandment: "Thou shalt not produce kitsch."

I wonder if this also works for music, photography, dance and sculpture. Give it a go, dear reader, and send me your results.

info@clearmindpress.com

Perspective and colour

Perspective in drawing is a technique used to represent three-dimensional objects on a two-dimensional surface, creating a realistic and three-dimensional illusion for the viewer. This technique is crucial in creating lifelike drawings, as it allows artists to show depth and distance on a flat surface. From a philosophical standpoint, perspective in drawing can be seen as a metaphor for how we perceive and comprehend the world. Like a well-constructed drawing, our perception of the world is shaped by our individual experiences, beliefs, and perspectives. When we view a drawing, we are not seeing the actual object, but rather a representation of it. Similarly, when we look at the world around us, we are not seeing the true reality, but rather our interpretation of it. Our perspective influences how we perceive and understand the world, just as the artist's perspective influences their drawing.

This does not imply that our perception of the world is entirely subjective, nor does it suggest that there is no objective truth. Nevertheless, it is important to acknowledge that our perspective influences how we comprehend and interpret the world around us. Therefore, it is crucial to consider multiple perspectives and remain receptive to alternative viewpoints to gain a more nuanced and accurate understanding of the world.

Colour is a crucial aspect of our visual experience of the world, and we often regard it as a fundamental property of the objects and scenes we perceive. However, the reality is that colour does not exist in the external world in the way we experience it. Instead, colour is an illusion generated by our brains in response to the wavelengths of light reflected off of objects and into our eyes. The visible spectrum of light, which we perceive as the colours of the rainbow, is just a small fraction of the full spectrum of electromagnetic radiation. When light of various wavelengths strikes an object, some are absorbed, and others are reflected. The wavelengths that reach our eyes are what we interpret as colour.

Thus, the colour of an object is not an inherent property of the object itself but rather a subjective interpretation by our brains based on the wavelengths of light that are reflected off of it.

An apple, for example, appears red to us because it absorbs all the wavelengths of light in the visible spectrum except the ones we perceive as red, which are reflected into our eyes. If we were to view the same apple under a different type of light, such as ultraviolet light, it would appear distinct to us because the wavelengths of ultraviolet light that are absorbed and reflected by the apple would be different.

In other words, our brains create the illusion of colour to interpret the information provided by our eyes. This is why colours can appear distinct under varying lighting conditions or when viewed by individuals with different types of colour vision. It's also why colours can seem different on different screens or in various media, such as paint or digital art.

While the illusion of colour may be a practical way of perceiving the world around us, it's crucial to remember that it's just that – an illusion. The world's true nature is defined by the underlying physical properties of the objects and scenes we perceive, not by the colours we see.

What do marks on paper do to us?

What effect do the marks on paper or canvas, known as drawings and paintings, have on us? Why do we hold them in such high regard? The answer to these questions varies from person to person. To better understand, we should split the inquiry into two parts: one that concerns the act of making marks, and the other that focuses on the act of appreciating the marks created by humans.

Why don't we consider marks made by animals or natural elements such as wind, or the marks left by a tree branch in the sand as art? There is an entire realm of often-overlooked art out there: the art of animals and animate and inanimate objects in nature. Why aren't the clear, slimy strings with pitch-black cane toad eggs drifting in water considered art? What about the marks made by a giraffe's teeth on a tree's bark?

Art appears to become art when it references something.

Additionally, there is l'art pour l'art, which is art that references only itself.

Certain human painters enjoy the process of making marks. Chris Tate, a painter discussed in another essay in this collection, has stated that the act of making marks brings him joy.

Conversely, I have always found drawing and painting to be arduous and unpleasant. Nevertheless, I continue to do it because I cannot live without it, for reasons that are explained elsewhere in this collection. In recent years, as I have grown older, drawing and painting have become less burdensome and more pleasurable. This transformation has taken fifty three years. My first paintings and drawings, which were intended to be "art" rather than a child's drawings, were created with great trepidation and uncertainty. I am unsure why, but my father's strong opinions, as he was a drawing and painting teacher, may have played a role.

I have never been particularly fond of my own drawings and paintings, but others consistently appreciate them. I am uncertain of the significance of this. It is just how it is. I frequently examine my drawings, particularly after completing them, but do not genuinely enjoy them. Instead, I am taken aback that they emerged from my hand, as if they are foreign entities.

Despite this, I continue to make them. I feel as though I am missing a limb when I do not draw. I have been drawing my entire life, so perhaps it is merely a habit, like having an arm or a mobile phone.

At one point, my childhood's drawings (which, by definition, are not art) transitioned into art. What was the difference? I am not attempting to provide an answer to that question; because questions are more intriguing than their answers.

The act of consuming art created by others is distinct. It serves as an escape route for me, especially during times when I despise humanity., which is often This is peculiar since art is produced solely by humans. I am not attempting to explain it; I only wish to document it. When the stupidity of humankind overwhelms me, I retreat into the realm of the arts and emerge feeling better. It's akin to taking an internal bath. It purifies me.

Dutch COBRA poet and painter Lucebert (1924-1994) wrote, "Alles van waarde is weerloos" ("Everything of value is defenseless") in his poem "De zeer oude zingt" ("The very old sings"). This line evokes numerous meanings, but it primarily pertains to that which is small and vulnerable, as it is the most valuable thing in existence. We read, "Wordt van aanraakbaarheid rijk" ("Become rich from touchability") in the same poem. We could interpret these words as a plea for the richness of vulnerability, the ability to allow oneself to be touched by others and to be receptive. Despite sounding paradoxical, such an attitude of vulnerability and imperfection necessitates much more courage than the pursuit of perfection.

In a society that idealizes perfection, it is not always apparent to focus on that which is unsightly or mundane. Leonard Cohen sings, "There's a crack in everything. That is where the light gets in." Not everyone is or can be who they would like to be. Small and large imperfections make individuals unique and approachable. The same might be said for art.

However, we must tread carefully when making such claims. Always. Whenever we say anything, we must tread lightly.

Life Drawing

I have always loved life drawing classes because they are places where the nude human body is not sexualized or judged, and its vulnerability is respected rather than objectified. One can always find good people in these classes, as creeps feel uncomfortable and leave.

There is often music playing to relax both the model and the drawers, creating an atmosphere of relaxed concentration and absorption. The sound of drawing is soothing: the touch of charcoal, pencil, crayon, or pen on paper.

The class follows a gentle discipline of sticking to pose times and pauses, ensuring that no time is wasted. Subtleties that are often overlooked in daily life are deemed important in life drawing, such as the light in the room, the temperature, and the way we move around, speak, or remain silent. It is a gently orchestrated world where time seems to stop or go on forever. It is a time capsule that gently embraces the participants as soon as they enter, feeling like a spaceship.

I've attended such classes all over the world, starting as a young model and later as an artist. They are similar everywhere, focusing on the drawing process rather than the final result. Some have a teacher, while many are run by a facilitator, and the sessions are always relatively affordable. Some organize regular exhibitions of the participants' work.

Life drawing classes are an excellent way for drawers to hone their skills and develop their ability to draw the human form, allowing them to practice studying the human body in various positions and poses. One of the essential skills learned is foreshortening, a technique to create the illusion of three-dimensional space on a two-dimensional surface. This is particularly useful in life drawing, as it allows the artist to depict the complex three-dimensional forms of the human body. Foreshortening involves using perspective to create the illusion of objects closer to the viewer appearing larger and objects farther away appearing smaller. This can be a challenging technique to master, but it is crucial for artists looking to improve their life drawing abilities.

One of the great benefits of attending a life drawing class is that it allows artists to practice their skills in a supportive and constructive environment. Instructors often are experienced drawers who can offer feedback and guidance to help students improve. To improve technical skills, life drawing classes can help artists develop their ability to observe and interpret. By studying the human form, artists learn to see beyond the surface level and capture the nuances and gestures that make each person unique.

Another benefit of life drawing classes is that they provide community and camaraderie. The classes are a great way to meet others and share ideas and techniques, which can help to inspire and motivate.

I feel at home in life drawing classes. I wish I could live full-time in them. I could easily spend all my time drawing the human form while soiling my clothes and hair with ink, pastels and paints while wearing two different socks in sandals under an old dress and occasionally burst into slightly- out-of-tune song when I recognise a tune. It is a hundred per cent my kind of thing.

I draw with ink, which does not allow for erasing or hiding mistakes. I make the ink myself by grinding burned walnut husk into a powder and mixing it with water, using an old European technique from the 16th century. It is called *bistre*.

The washi paper I use I made over thirty years ago in a Zen monastery in Japan. I made a thousand sheets in the 1980ies during a silent retreat over four months. I have been moving the dwindling stack with me from country to country for nearly forty years. It will be a sad day when I run out of this magnificent paper.

Chris Tate

It's funny that because of my condition and the nature of pastels, I find myself almost being - pardon the pun - drawn along, sometimes like on a sleigh ride, directed by gravity and an unknown wind. (Chris Tate, in an email on 19 November 2022).

Chris Tate is a painter in England. Eschewing influences from other painters and art forms, Tate (1951) paints what his brain communicates to his hand. He interferes as little as possible in this process. The results are remarkably fresh, strangely familiar and surprisingly consistent.

Until a few years ago, Tate has been a writer. He has always been interested in painters and their work, but believed that he himself would be completely incompetent as a painter. However, at a certain point in his life, in his mid-sixties, he felt that he wanted to paint.

Soon after he had started painting, Tate discovered that he had fallen victim to a crippling chronic illness that made painting nearly impossible. Sometimes, his hands refused to hold a brush. Nevertheless, he persevered.

He noticed that his paintings and drawings were

like a child's, and were not developing further. He felt he had to be both a critic and a defender of his own work. But while his effort to keep painting brought home the severity of his condition, actually producing the work also brought him a great deal of pleasure. So he kept going.

It took years for him to take seriously what his hands were creating. At first, he critiqued his own work using the same eye-rolling terms that any unreflective observer might have used: "My three-year-old could do that," etc.

Thankfully, he did not throw his work away, but stored it in stacks. Slowly, he began to recognise its value. Marks on paper. Unplanned. Unique but universal. Archetypal. A process rather than a product.

Over the years, he tried working in several media: acrylic paint, iPad Paint, watercolours and pastels. The carrier, too, varied over time: linen, canvas, aquarelle paper, sugar paper…

> "I do the pastels on what was called "sugar paper" at primary school. Different coloured sheets, of the kind of paper, I think, that was initially used to wrap sugar, though I could be wrong. I certainly first saw pastels at primary school, in conjunction with sugar paper, which was why I got it. I must have had both pastels and paper for at least three years before I used them." (email 2 December 2022).

His body could hardly move to produce the marks, but it didn't seem to matter. Tate would leave a mark even if he could only make a crayon roll over the paper, for example, by blowing it forwards.

The stack of work kept growing.

As the works are all dated, Tate began to see them as diary entries, a record of the moves and marks he made on that day. This certainly reflected uncertainty about their place or worth in the world. "I'm over that now," Tate says, "it's too late for all that. Though I still find the question of what to do with them quite fascinating. A book, I think, is a perfect solution. Well before the Covid lockdown, my friend's daughter helped me put together a collection of my iPad drawings for one of those books you can get printed online…"

At first, Tate tried to give the works names, as artists do, but a friend (me) found that cheesy. Then he numbered them. But that did not feel right either.

What did feel right, though, was assigning them unrelated short descriptions, as from a radio play: "the sound of hooves on sand approaching". "The sound of glass breaking…"

This somewhat synaesthetic approach seems to stick. (Synaesthesia is a perceptual phenomenon in which stimulation of one sensory or cognitive pathway leads to involuntary experiences in a second sensory or cognitive pathway. People with synaesthesia may 'hear colours' or 'smell sounds'.)

"You [Suzanne] alerted me to the arbitrary nature

of naming paintings. Because I watch a lot of TV with subtitles, I began to be intrigued by the phrases describing sounds and started making a list. I wondered how they could help a deaf person. Presumably only by accessing memory, unless the person was deaf from birth, then a great leap of imagination would be needed. As these phrases were read, were part of the daily life around the pastels, I thought they might make amusing titles. Here are a couple:

She sobs quietly
Dog barking in the distance
Sombre orchestral music

It saves me from having to think up phrases!"

Sometimes, Tate's work resembles Australian Aboriginal paintings: those of Kudditji Kngwarreye, for example, or Minnie Pwerle. They have the same kind of uninhibited open-mindedness.

Looking and seeing

To be a skilled drawer or painter, one must learn how to truly see. The act of looking and seeing is an art form in itself. If painting or drawing is not the result of observation, but rather imagination alone, it can easily become kitsch. In my opinion, Salvador Dali is the ultimate master of kitsch, as his art is entirely born from his imagination without any true observation of the world around him. People who are fond of Dali often have certain characteristics; they may also enjoy Pink Floyd and believe in conspiracy theories and UFOs. The reason for this combination remains a mystery to me.

The process of looking and seeing is a complex one. For example, if I cut a shape out of a white piece of paper and place it back onto the same white paper, I will not see the shape. However, if I crumple the shape slightly, some parts of it will float slightly off the paper, and I will see the shape. This is because the shadow beneath the shape gives it definition against the background.

When we observe things, we are always looking at two things at once: the object and its background. The difference between the figure and the background gives the figure its identity. We can only experience an object or figure by comparing it with something else. Thus, seeing and looking are essentially acts of distinguishing.

It is impossible to see or look at the essence of a thing. We never see things directly.

The passage of time also plays a role in what we see. When we observe a nearby object, we see it in almost real-time, despite the fact that it takes a fraction of a second for the image to travel from our eyes to our brain. When we observe objects that are very far away, such as stars, we see a version of them that existed a long time ago. In this way, we look into the past when we observe the universe. Some objects that we see in the sky do not exist any longer.

Looking at things very closely, such as through a microscope, results in an even more bewildering experience. We encounter a world that is entirely unknown to us.

Closer to home, in our daily lives, there must be a relationship between two things before we can perceive or observe them. If we depict or describe something as a separate entity, we face a contradiction. Something cannot be both a thing and a relationship. So, what is it? We notice the figure, and we notice the background. What we see is the difference. Everything manifests itself through difference. Everything *is* difference.

There are no things or figures. We cannot see a single blade of grass in a lawn. Only when we place the blade of grass in another environment, such as on a white piece of paper, can we see it.

Dali paints as if there were things, not relationships. He calls this surrealism, but in reality, it is kitsch.

The fact that we have names for things and figures makes it easier for us to differentiate between them. It is impossible to draw something that we have never seen before, like Dali does, and that we do not know the name of.

People are generally somewhat scared of things they do not know. For his exams sculpting at Art Academy, my son made some unidentifiable man-sized blobs in silicon. He placed them in a public space and filmed what happened to them. First, the blobs were tentatively probed by people in the street. When the blobs did not fight back, they were attacked and destroyed. The film of this process was my son's artwork, not the blobs. So mother, so son.

In language, (wo)mankind can identify things as things. Dali uses painting and drawing as a language. He tells a story. The result could be better. It is kitsch. Or, if one wants to say something positive about it: it is illustration.

Language comes after looking and seeing. It separates things for our better understanding. Take the phenomenon of big and small. Things are only big or small in relation to each other. Once they have a name, they become seemingly separate entities. Big and small do not exist in painting or drawing. There are only relationships.

The translation of the perception of the senses into symbols is language. The translation of the perception of the senses into marks on paper is drawing or painting. A painter like Dali confuses the two. His paintings are often called "symbolic". Whatever people call them, I would so very much like to hit someone I dislike with a canvas by Dali so that the head of the disliked person comes crashing straight through the canvas.

Language is good at 'thinging' things. We look at a landscape: one thing. We describe it with words: there is a 'mountain' and a 'valley'. As if they are two separate things. They are not. The mountain cannot exist without the valley and vice versa. From one world, ten thousand things spring, just by naming them. Ten billion things spring from them when the ten thousand things are named. Language makes things multiply.

Looking and seeing makes things into one.
When language enters the picture, duality is born. Not only are there ten billion things to describe, but these things have all sorts of qualities; they are ugly or beautiful, big or small. Dali's paintings are ugly only because there are beautiful paintings like those of Rembrandt or Kamagurka to compare them with.

Reality is the world that the senses perceive before language has categorized it into a billion pieces, the non-dual and relational world. This world is presented to us through good paintings and drawings, not through kitsch ones. The world created by language and its symbols is, in a way, an artificial and second-hand world. The world of the senses is closer to 'reality,' whatever that may be. A table is a table thanks to all other objects that are not tables. The same applies to chairs, flowers, teapots, shoes, and beds. These objects owe their existence to other objects. Naming things creates a world of things with symbols attached to them. Pieces of reality are given names and become separate entities. These entities become images, such as a landscape, a garden, a body, or an interior. These, in turn, lead to styles in drawing and painting, such as still life, life drawing, flowers, hunting, portraits, and more. This process of naming and categorizing reality is (wo)mankind's way of seeking reality. It is what makes us human.

The difficulty of perceiving more than one thing simultaneously is illustrated by the famous image of the vase/faces. We tend to see either the vase or the faces, even if we are aware that both are present.

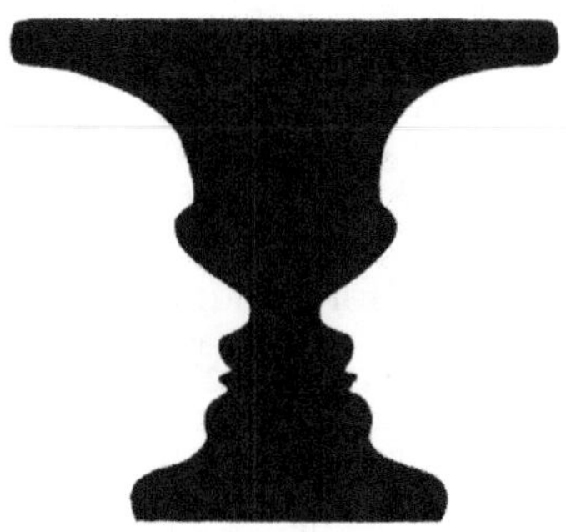

An interesting phenomenon is repetition. PickAsshole said that repetition does not comply with the laws of the human mind. We can only perceive repetition if it is spread out and occurs in different places. It is because of the difference in location that we can distinguish one repetition from another. Some artists play with this idea. Andy Asshole comes to mind.

Monotony and repetition are seen as unpleasant by most people. Punishment in prisons relies on this fact. When there is too much repetition and monotony, for example, eating Campbell soup for breakfast, lunch, and dinner seven days a week, people hallucinate to make up for the boredom.

People who draw or paint are vaguely to very conscious of these realities. They are on a quest to experience, record, and uncover reality. There is a subtle difference between discovering and uncovering. What do things really look like? That things look different from what we think they look like becomes clear when we study perspective and foreshortening or the dimensions of the human body. An open hand is as big as a face. This is surprising to many. The human body is about five to six times the height of its head. A good drawer pays as much attention to the foreground, the subject, and the background while not separating them too drastically.

Whether a figure, such as a model in life drawing, is ugly or beautiful is irrelevant to the artist. Ugly and beautiful belong to the world of language, not the world of looking. The world has not yet split into ugly things and beautiful things when simply looking and seeing. Things just are what they are. Are there ugly trees and beautiful trees? Ugly landscapes and beautiful landscapes? Ugly sunsets and beautiful sunsets? If so, what determines their ugliness and beauty? I enjoy it when an essay ends with a question.

Questions are often more interesting than answers.

Looking, a short but rather precise observation

I have learned that I am looking out of two slits: my eyes. Yet my experience is different. I am not looking out of two restrictive small mailboxes into a boxed-in world. Instead, when I look, I seem to have, or rather *be*, one big open eye that looks out into the world. That eye resides where my head is supposed to be.

To experience this clearly, I form a pair of glasses with my hands. I form two circles with my thumbs and forefingers. I hold these circles next to each other to resemble a pair of glasses. I move these "glasses" towards my nose as if I want to put them on. At first, I see two holes approaching my eyes. But when I "put" them onto my face and look through them, I don't see two holes; I see one wide-open space that I am looking into and out of.

Similarly, I can create a paper mask with the eyes cut out. As soon as I put on the mask, I don't see slits but one open space that I am looking out of into the world. The world does not "stop" at the surface of my face but penetrates me. It is both there *and* here, within me, and there is no distance between the "two".

When I think that I am looking from two slits called eyes, I mistake the first person for the third person. Most people have these slits, so I must have them too. However, the first-person experience is quite different.

When I look down at my body, I see my legs, feet, arms, and my chest ends where my vision ends, and the one big open eye begins. I can't see my head. Where my head is supposed to be, there is the world that I see. The world appears in that big open eye, that capacity for the ever-changing world, including my body.

This indicates that I am not in my body, but my body is in me! I have cracked my shell. I'm out of the box. I am free.

Note, too, that my feet are at the top of the page in the drawing. This indicates that I am upside down. A good observer will see this. Take a photograph of yourself sitting, down your body and tell me what you see. Are the feet at the top of the page?

What if I'm standing? My feet must go down when I'm standing for sure!

Nope, still upside down. Note: this only counts for the first person.

When I am in a landscape and spread my arms to "hold" the view and see my hands sticking out into the view, there is no distance. What is out there is also *here*, in me. I am in that landscape, and that landscape is in me. I am aware of the vastness there, which is also here, in me. I am "born to be wide".

I am capacity for the world. I look at the world

from deep within me. The point from where I'm looking is zero distance away from me.

I see the world, which is out there, *and* in me. There is no distance. There are no two worlds.

All I see is me.

My nose is huge! When I close one eye and look at it, it blocks part of my view. When my eyes are open, my brains cancel out this little inconvenience by filling in the blanks.

When I follow my nose, or the temples of my glasses, toward myself, I end up in a void. There's no one sitting there, in the middle of my skull, a little me, looking through my slits that are called eyes.

There's no one there. There's only looking. There's no "I" that's looking. This is the concept of No-Self in Zen.

Science is not finding an "I" either. With this in mind, next time you draw, ask yourself: who's drawing? And: Where are my feet? And: how big is my nose today?

It takes two to tango, always two

I'm in my car, seeing my hands on the steering wheel and feeling my body glued to the chair. My head is not visible to me. I'm aware of the big, wide-open eye that I'm using to look around. The car feels like an extension of me, responding to my every desire just like my arms and hands. Once I choose my destination and start driving, I see the world unfolding around me. The landscape or cityscape pours into me, and I remain still, one big open eye in which everything moves.

The trees close to me move backward, while those far away, near the horizon, move forward.

Movement through space is a complex phenomenon. Imagine you have one ball suspended in space, and then you add another ball. This second ball moves towards the first ball, or does it? Which ball is moving toward which? All we know is that there is linear motion. Adding a third ball introduces motion on a plane, while adding a fourth ball introduces motion in space (three dimensions). The motion is relative to the other balls. To have motion, we need at least two things.

Anything requires two things to happen. This is the essence of the famous "sound-of-the-clapping-of-one-hand" koan in Zen. The universe needs a brain to create reality. Without a brain, there is no reality.

Reality cannot exist in isolation. It needs to be observed. Everything we see, hear, touch, taste, and smell are waves (light waves, sound waves, etc.) that are interpreted and translated by our brain. Without the brain, there would be no light, colour, sound, or motion.

Thus, we, with our brains, co-create reality.

Even a simple drive turns out to be a mystery. Destinations come to us, landscapes pour in and out, and trees move in two directions. Reality is stranger than fiction.

Marks draw us

Neurophysiologist Benjamin Libet famously conducted experiments in the 1980s to investigate the neural underpinnings of conscious decision-making. His experiments were some of the earliest to propose that our brains may decide before we become consciously aware. In one study, participants were instructed to perform a simple action, such as pushing a button, while their brain activity was recorded via electroencephalography (EEG). Libet discovered that activity in the motor cortex, a region linked with movement, could be identified around half a second before the participants reported having made the decision to push the button. These results have been interpreted by some as evidence contradicting the existence of free will, as they suggest that our actions are predetermined by neural activity rather than conscious choice.

When we face a blank piece of paper and begin to draw something, our hands instinctively make decisions before we even realize it. We then take credit for the marks and say that we "did the drawing". The stronger our belief in our free will behind our mark-making, the larger our signature becomes, often ruining the drawing.

It's entirely mysterious who drew the drawing. Drawing is like a door to a vast mystery that keeps unfolding like a flower opening. One thing is certain: we are not the ones "doing the drawing". Instead, the marks on the paper draw us. Feeling this mystery makes us feel alive. This is why drawing is so alluring or even addictive. We feel the vastness and contradiction that lies beyond it, urging us to continue. Without it, life can seem flat and one-dimensional once we've experienced it.

The feeling of being drawn doesn't just apply to drawing. Dancer Tanaka Min once said that he was danced by his surroundings, whether it be the room he was in or the wind when he danced outside. I also recall saying, when I was still able to move freely, that I danced the dance the body remembers. Ernest Hemingway, a writer known for saying that his books wrote themselves, believed that the characters and events in his stories already existed and that he simply transcribed them. Musician Jimi Hendrix similarly claimed that his instrument played itself. The world of arts suffered when personality became its main focus. The cult of personality has not always been a part of it. Rembrandt, for instance, was a craftsman who painted for anyone who needed a portrait of themselves or a group to which they belonged. The current cult of personality in the arts stems from the monetary, power, or sexual value of art. It is the least genuine and least interesting aspect of art. Figures like Andy Asshol and

Jeff Koons come to mind, whose personalities overshadow the art they created. PickAsshole may be an exception, as his work was as significant as his personality, power, and sexual cult.

Those who remain humble and avoid the injuries of the arts are moved by the mystery of the marks that draw us.

When I first faced this virtual paper this morning, I had no idea what would happen. I only had a vague plan. Once my fingers hit the keyboard, the writing began to unfold on its own. I had no idea what the next line would be. The words came together and formed sentences like pearls on a string. My hands strung them together while my mind observed. I'm not sure how or when it will end, but it will end. And now, it seems that it has ended.

This is how we write and draw.

Dynamic drawing

An ode to Ron Curran

My father was a teacher of drawing and painting, but he didn't teach me much. Instead, he instilled in me a fear of making mistakes and doing it wrong. When I was around twenty-three, he told me that I "could not draw" and advised me to give up because I was not suited for it. Nevertheless, I persisted in drawing.

A fortunate moment occurred twenty years later, far from my father, in wild and sunny Australia, where I met Ron Curran. It was the year 2000, and I had just relocated to Australia. A friend of mine was taking drawing lessons from a teacher named Ron Curran in Byron Bay, Lismore, and Mullumbimby, and I decided to join her. It was under Ron 's guidance that I truly learned what drawing is all about. It was there that I discovered my voice and my language. Ron taught a wildly popular class called Dynamic Drawing, which continues to draw full classes of 20 to 30 students to this day.

In the class, we always had a model for life drawing, but it was much more than that. During the first half-hour, we only did short poses that lasted for a minute at most.

We drew with our eyes closed, the wrong hand, upside down, two hands, the space around the model, or the model in one line - there was no time to think.

Ron was always encouraging, speaking poetically, and facilitating a transformation in everyone. The art produced in his classes was phenomenal.

I immediately noticed a difference in the drawings I produced. They were better, fresher, and unique. It was like developing a language instead of just creating drawings.

Ron says on his website:

> "We all have our language. For most of us the language is already there; it's just a question of good strategy, accessing those structures and effectively overcoming our resident fears. The language isn't always just sitting there in our hand; we have to work at it to uncover and to meet ourselves. We need to remind ourselves that the whole history of art is a history of diversity and difference — if it were not, there would be no history of art. To learn to sit on one's signature and draw from that place in a structured and focused way is to embrace drawing in a far more meaningful and total way — to allow your stories to meet the stories of the world around you."

I stayed with Ron for over three glorious years, learning about marks on paper. I drew in old Bibles, on maps, in dictionaries, and even with old makeup. Occasionally, I went to the pharmacy to collect out-of-date skin foundation.

I attended Ron's class twice or three times a week, driving long distances in my old Holden Camira between Byron Bay, Mullumbumbi, and Lismore. These were the highlights of my week.

I made fascinating friends in the class, who are still incredible drawers and painters, most notably Marion Patricia Douglas and Sergio Tores Pacheco.

After that long and satisfying immersion in Ron's classes, I was prepared to face the world of drawing alone, and I have never stopped drawing since. Ron was the beginning of my freedom in mark-making.

His teaching was deeply connected to other concepts, such as the need to consume versus the desire to be free from that need and the right to return home to oneself. It was profoundly meaningful and anarchistic.

Ron marked the beginning of my true venture into the realm of real drawing. I remember those years with great fondness, the time when I discovered my authentic handwriting. Ron brought out the best in me, not just in drawings but also in other aspects of my life.

"By admitting our vulnerabilities, by returning to our original state of innocence, our seeing begins and it is in this state of surrender that our stories begin.

We can maybe start to get clear, to make a claim on reality, attempt some kind of restoration or resolution and touch upon our real identity. Everybody looking for their signature, everyone looking for their words, everyone looking for 'their writing'."
Ron Curran.

Thank you, Ron! What an incredible experience I had with you. I am now a part of a life drawing group in Alice Springs and was also a part of one in Maryborough, Queensland when my studies took me to Hervey Bay. Now and then I meet someone who also attended your classes. We speak of you fondly and with great respect and love.

How not to write about art

The following essay grew from a collaboration between Chris Tate, Jonathan Smith and Suzanne Visser, long-term friends bound by a number of elements: Japan (they lived there), language (they write) and food (they like fine dining). They also like to reflect and occasionally bitch about things.

Suzanne:

I don't like the word "create". It is just another word for "make". The word "create" has been abused by artists and critics alike, and because of this it has an odour to it: it smells of pretension. I prefer words such as build, construct, fabricate, form, generate, produce, execute, shape…or, even better, using the verb connected to the art form: draw, paint, sculpt, sing, photograph, dance, play an instrument….

Jonathan:

I really dislike "Creative", as a collective noun. As in "she works in performance spaces with other creatives."

Why? Because this too reeks of pretension. It sets up apartheid between People Who Are Creative (us) and the rest of humanity: We are creative, you are not. Creativity is our job, not yours; when you need some creativity then give us the work, because only we can be taken seriously. More subtly, it sets up a false, circular definition: it implies that creativity is what "Creatives" engage in.

Well, Creatives: software engineers, those nerdy people you probably don't notice, are being creative every day. So are parents. So kindly don't hijack and ring-fence the word to make it applicable only to what you do.

For me, to "express oneself (through art)" is also off-limits. Does the butcher express himself by cutting nice slices of meat? Does the shoe repairer express himself through sewing strong seams? Why on earth are artists understood to be "expressing" themselves? Is a drawing an expression? And if so, of what precisely? The drawer's mood?

Chris:

This "creative" nonsense has been going on for decades. I remember in the early 70s, I came across the notion of "creativity" in schools, and thought it was the biggest load of bollocks.

Who, in a sense, isn't creative? And to restrict it to the field of so-called "art" was the icing on the cake. In those days, the unspoken consensus in schools was that science subjects were somehow inferior to arts subjects, not including painting, but English, languages and history. You weren't creative in maths. Physics was for nerds. It seems a long way from that to today's situation where certain people like to identify as "creative", as if it makes them special.

As for painting being self-expression, definitely not. I increasingly see painting as a process of problem-solving, arriving at a certain collection of colour and shape, and then going on to find an acceptable arrangement, which may include some unconscious retrieval. It doesn't have anything to do with how my mother may have treated me when I was five or how X broke my heart later.

I think a big difference between this generation and ours is that we took a more existential approach, that life was finite, and to find meaning in that was part of the task, you defined your stay on those terms. Today identity comes from reacting to social media. The individual is a reaction to technology. Perhaps it's always been like that, but not in the all-pervasive way of now.

We asked AI to write the concluding paragraph of this essay. This is what it came up with:

In conclusion, when it comes to writing about art, it's important to be mindful of the language and terminology we use. Words like "create" and "creative" can be loaded with pretension and create unnecessary divisions between those who are deemed "creative" and those who are not. Likewise, the notion of art as self-expression can be limiting and simplistic. Instead, we should focus on the process of problem-solving and the technical skills required to produce art. At the same time, we need to be open to new ways of approaching art and finding meaning in the world around us. Ultimately, writing about art should be about fostering a deeper understanding and appreciation of the creative process, rather than perpetuating cliches and stereotypes.

When we asked AI to make it wittier and more interesting, it came up with this:

When it comes to writing about art, it's important to keep your language palette as diverse and exciting as the art itself. Words like "create" can be as stale as last week's baguette and using them too much can make you sound like a pretentious cheese-lover. Instead, why not spice things up with verbs like build, sculpt, or fabricate? You'll be the life of the party, and your writing will be fresher than a farmers' market bouquet.

And let's not forget about "creative," the word that's been hijacked by art world snobs and self-proclaimed visionaries. Using it as a collective noun is as cringeworthy as wearing socks with sandals. It's time to break down the walls between "creatives" and everyone else and recognize that creativity is not the sole domain of artists. Software engineers can be creative, as can parents and butchers.

So, let's leave the word "creative" for what it really is: a vague and overused label that's best left to the marketing department.

Finally, the notion that art is all about self-expression is about as deep as a kiddie pool. We should move beyond this simplistic view and recognize that art is often a process of problem-solving and technical skill.

Creating a masterpiece is more like a game of chess than a therapy session. Of course, there's always room for personal expression in art, but let's not forget about the other factors that go into making great art. So, let's raise our glasses (or paintbrushes) to a new era of art writing that's bold, witty, and full of flavour.

Cheers!

Seeing

"God gave you a face and you made yourself another."
William Shakespeare (Hamlet)

Most of the time, we see what we think is there, and we do not see things as they really are. This is because we have the habit of seeing ourselves as a third person rather than a first person. We see other people with a body, limbs, neck, and head, and then we project this image onto ourselves. However, we cannot see our own neck, head, or certain parts of our chest and back. When we see ourselves as we truly are, in the first person, we look like this.

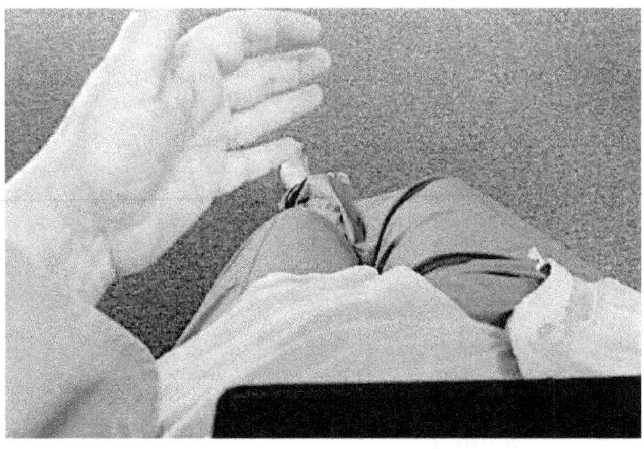

This is what I look like to myself. As you can see, I have no head. My hand is big. My feet are tiny. I'm upside down. My feet are at the top. Can't see it? Draw this picture and you will see. The feet are at the top of your page.

We can only see our own face (neck, chest, backside) in a mirror. In reality, our face is everywhere except where we expect it to be. It is visible as a reflection in mirrors and shiny surfaces such as windows, TV screens, and spoons. Where we expect to see our face, there is nothing to be seen.

You can experience this firsthand by pointing at things.

First, point at something random in the room, like a shoe by the door. Take note of the experience: its color, texture, size, etc.

Then, point at something closer to your body, like a chair. Take note of the experience: its color, texture, size, etc. This does not take long.

Next, point at your own knee and do the same: texture, color, size.

Finally, point at your own chest. The experience becomes slightly stranger. Your chest does not look like the chests of other people, nor like what you have learned a chest is supposed to look like. Instead, it is a shapeless thing that moves up and down under a layer of clothing, like a sleeping animal.

Then point at your face and ask yourself: "What am I pointing at?"

Something strange happens. You are now pointing at something you cannot see. You are pointing into a kind of void. You are pointing at nothing. No thing.

To myself, I have no face. Only to others do I have a face. Of course, I can see my face in a mirror; my face is then literally on the surface of the mirror. In fact, my face is everywhere - in the mirror, on other shiny surfaces such as windows, TV screens, and spoons - except where it is supposed to be.

Where my face is supposed to be is an openness from where I am looking, or rather, from where looking is happening.

I resist this truth. Others don't look like that, so why should I? I quickly "thing" myself to fit in. But the reality is that the first person (I) is completely different from the third person (you).

There are several painters and drawers who have played with this strange phenomenon.

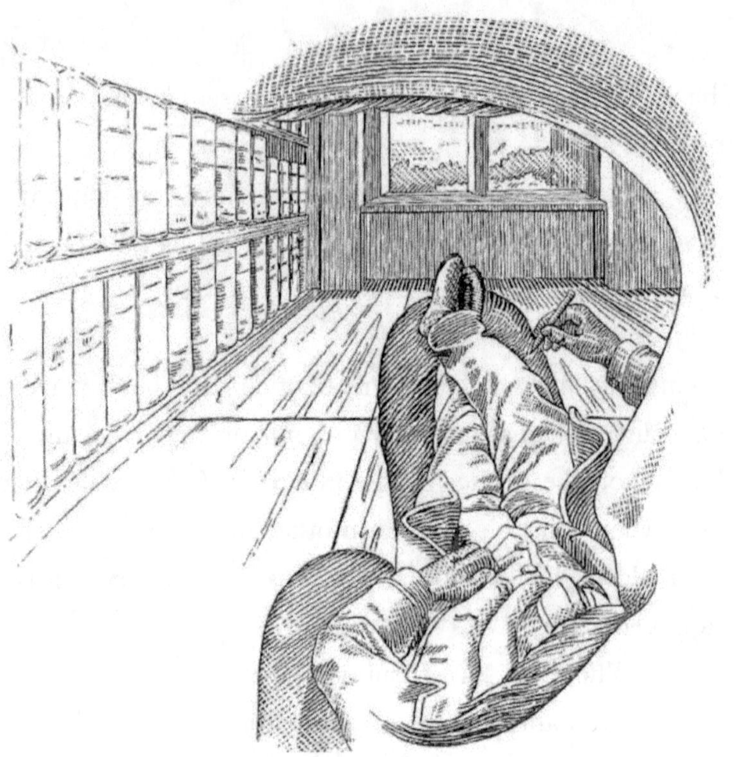

Mach draws reality as it is. He has no head. His nose and eyebrow are huge and opaque and come out of nowhere. He is upside down: His feet are on top.

In many paintings by the Belgian painter Roger Raveel, the figures have no face. Raveel also often portrays the head as an empty space. There are several self-portraits by Raveel that are seen from the first person's view.

A baby looks from the first person's perspective. It has not "thinged" (objectified) itself yet. This perspective continues for about two to two and a half years. The toddler turns around the arrow of attention and "things" (objectifies) itself. This has been tested by painting a red dot on the child's nose and having them look in the mirror. When the child points at the red dot in the mirror, they have not "thinged" (objectified) themselves yet. When the child points at its own nose, it has "thinged" (objectified) itself. The British philosopher and architect Douglas Harding wrote many books on "having no head". The realization that one does not have a face (nor a head) to oneself has many implications. "Thinging" (objectifying) oneself is painful. One becomes one of the Ten Thousand Things (an object; nothing special) if one "things" (objectifies) oneself. Not "thinging" (objectifying) oneself makes one more in line with reality and part of it.

We do not look out into the world through the two slits we see in others (eyes). Instead, we are looking from a wide-open window, so to speak. We perceive this "window" we are looking out of or from as oval in shape. Things at the periphery of this oval are blurred, except when we move our eyes toward the edges, then they appear sharper.

An interesting question now arises: Who is the one looking from this openness? We can try to find that person (I) by pointing into the emptiness where our face is supposed to be and ask ourselves again: Who or what am I pointing at? The answer is clear and astonishing: I am pointing at nothing, at no thing, at no one!

There is a British man named Richard Laing who travels the world to make people aware of this strange and thought-provoking phenomenon. He is a student of the late Douglas Harding, the English architect and philosopher who wrote *On Having No Head.*

When we look and see what we think is there, we ignore distance. We usually see each other from a certain distance, and we use this image when we think of ourselves or others. This distance is about three meters so that we can see the whole person, from the feet to the top of the head. This is a static and incorrect assumption.

Things, people, and animals change dramatically as our distance to them changes. When we zoom out, a person seen from one kilometer looks like the house they are in. From 100,000 kilometers, they look like the earth. From a billion kilometers, they look like a star. When zooming in, a similar transformation happens. As we step closer to a person, we may see some patch of opaque skin. Closer still, we see skin cells. Then we see the interior of cells and end up in the nucleus, which is strangely empty, like the universe around a star or the void we point into when pointing at where our face is supposed to be.

Being aware of these phenomena is beneficial to painting and drawing.

We are not like a camera lens recording. We are looking and seeing in constant flux. There's no one who is looking. Looking just happens from that void where our face is supposed to be. We *are* looking and seeing.

Good drawers and painters instinctively know this. They hardly take credit for their drawings or paintings. Paintings and drawings just happen. No one is drawing or painting.

Taking credit

An awkward situation arises when someone compliments an artist's work. What is one supposed to say? "Thank you"? But that would imply taking credit for something that is given to us. It's as if my aunt had gifted me a beautiful handmade sweater, and someone says, "Great sweater, you are very talented," and I reply, "Thank you." What I should say is, "But I haven't done anything! My hand has drawn or written something, and I'm as surprised as anybody else about what has landed on the paper. I had a vague plan that I abandoned almost immediately while drawing (or writing) because the drawing (or story) took over as soon as I began. It, the drawing (the story), dictates what I have to do next."

For example, the drawing says, "Now you need to move your pencil/charcoal/brush to that corner because it feels neglected."

Or the story may say, "Walk around this person. It is too two-dimensional." Or it may say, "Slow down, give the story some air. It is far too dense..."

Those who cannot hear the voice of the drawing (or the story) need teachers, editors, and agents. They need others to intervene, give directions, ask the right questions, or say the right things to get a good drawing (or story) done. Editors, teachers, and agents then speak instead of the drawing (or the story): "You need a bit more color here," or "You need to develop this character."

The crux lies in becoming one's own teacher, editor, and agent; only then can one create authentic work. Once one stops listening to teachers, editors, and agents and begins listening to the drawing (or the story), one may make something worthwhile keeping.

A painting once begged me to give a figure in it a blue arm. I did what the painting demanded and painted the figure's arm blue. Then the compliments started: "Great painting. That blue arm is brilliant." At this point, I could say, "Thank you, but it was the painting's idea to have a blue arm. I just listened and followed its direction." "Thank you, but it was the painting that did it. It was the painting that screamed out, 'Paint that arm blue.' I couldn't not listen."

I know this sounds crazy, but it's the truth. My decision to put certain marks on paper was already made before it became conscious. This is a scientific fact. Something was drawing, or rather, drawing was happening, and when I realized what was happening, I took credit for it and said that I was the one who drew the drawing and made the arm blue. But who or what really drew it? The answer is bizarre: Nobody. Nobody drew the drawing (or told the story). There was just drawing (or storytelling) happening. They were already there, the drawings (the stories). They just needed to be uncovered. They lay dormant until someone found them, like a treasure.

One can find the strange game of compliment-giving-and-receiving on artists' Facebook pages. For example, a photographer posts a nice photo that is more than a snapshot, a photo that is meant to be "art," and people begin to comment:

Friend: "Great photo."

Artist: "Thank you."

Another friend: "Brilliant composition."

Artist: "Thank you."

Yet another friend: "You are talented."

Artist: "Thank you."

Friend of a friend: "Great timing."

Artist: "Thank you."

This goes on forever. It is the lamest thing ever.

I refuse to play that game. I don't want to say thank you. Not because I am a cantankerous old artist, but because I cannot take credit for something that's not mine but was instead given to me as a present. By whom or what this present was given (talent, cleverness, a good drawing, a good story), I do not know. Some may call it "God," others may call it "nature," and yet others will call it "the universe"...

The truth is that nobody knows where the natural ability to draw, to shoot good photos, to "have talent"... comes from. One thing is certain: I did not cause it. Nobody knows what "talent" is. We recognize it when we see it, but what is it? It seems to have a genetic component (nature) to it. My father was a teacher of drawing, for example. There must be some nurture involved too.... There is a whole teaching of the arts industry after all.

However, who or what gives us that ultimate present that is an authentic work of art? Nobody knows! Or rather, nobody does! An authentic artwork creates itself from no-thing. First, there was nothing, and then there was this thing. This is incredibly mysterious. We witness this mystery when we agree that an artwork is great.

To put a human signature on it is, well, reducing the mystery.

It is working with this mystery that Rembrandt, Serra, Neil Young, Robert Saltzman, David Bowie, Le Corbusier, David Byrne, PickAsshole, Roger Raveel, Frans Hals, Charlie Parker, Leonard Cohen, Degas, John Coltrane, Isamu Noguchi, Laurie Anderson, Cezanne, James Brown, and thousands of others have in common.

They know or knew how to read their medium humbly. They listen(ed) to their song (drawing, design, painting, sculpture, photograph) and let it dictate the way.   I have never believed in the cult of the artist as a person, and I know that, for example, the photographer

Robert Saltzman changed his career as a photographer because of it. A bit more about this in the next essay.

The role of money, power and sex and the cult of personality in the arts

The field of the arts was injured by the rise of capitalism and its consumerism. Even groups and individuals who protested against the rise of consumerism, such as John Lennon and Yoko Ono, profited immensely from the very thing they protested against. Pop music became the most consumed form of art from the 1960s onwards. Powerful singers promoted sex with very young girls ("If her daddy is rich, take her out for a meal, if her daddy's poor just do as you feel," Mungo Jerry. "'Oh baby, it's a wild world. I'll always remember you as a child, girl," by Cat Stevens), and often promoted heavy drinking, drug use, and destroying hotel rooms... in short, hedonism was rife. Contemporary art underwent a less noisy but similar hedonistic development. Unbelievable prices were and are paid for random artists' work whose value is decided by random but influential critics. This has had a ripple effect that has not benefited the arts and its reputation.

Old male artists often date underage female models to show off at their vernissage, where champagne and sushi are consumed while looking at the latest farts of the artist on the walls. Art critics, who are masters of woolly language, describe the artworks in expensive magazines full of advertisements for expensive products. Stupid art collectors pay millions to increase their power and sex appeal in this world of smoke and mirrors. The language of this world has infected the arts.

"As I sauntered into the gallery at the vernissage, I was immediately struck by the grandeur of the exhibition before me. The paintings, each a unique and magnificent work of art, seemed to radiate a sense of sophistication that left me utterly enraptured. The paintings lured me in, seducing me and rejecting me at the same time. The brushstrokes, bold and striking, spoke to the artist's unrivalled inspiration, talent, and ingenuity. The use of color was nothing short of divine, with each shade perfectly chosen to elevate and enrich the overall composition, which seemed to hide a deep secret. But it was not just the technical prowess of the paintings that impressed me. No, it was the profound and thought-provoking themes behind each work that truly made this exhibition so incredible. One painting in particular, a portrait of a regal figure surrounded by luxurious accoutrements, spoke to the timeless and universal themes of money, power, and wealth. The way the light danced across the figure's face, illuminating their pained expression, was a true testament to the artist's ability to capture the very essence of extravagance. It drew me in and touched the soul deep within me, then it spit me out again in disdain, it seemed, as in a confronting play with the viewer's psyche.

Overall, the exhibition was a true masterpiece, and I left feeling both awestruck, humiliated, and intellectually stimulated. It is clear that the artist is a true visionary, and I eagerly await their next opus."

This idiotic language has been around for so long now that it has become the norm. It turns people who did not grow up with it away from the arts. A cult of the artist as a personality goes with it. Andy Asshole is, of course, the ultimate example. The whole world bought him and is still buying him. A recent Netflix miniseries about him bears witness to this fact. I am not saying he had no talent, there was a little bit, but the attention he received was so disproportionate that any attempt to take him seriously became obsolete. Artists began portraying themselves as spoiled brats, having fits when something was not to their liking, whining when their sensitive soul was insulted by a critic, and crying when the well of "inspiration" dried up... This image of the artist as a spoiled brat has greatly damaged less famous but often better artists.

Art has, of course, nothing to do with money and the power and sex that goes with it. Great art must often be made alone in a studio or writer's room, far away from all that madness.

Many artists are poor because there are too many

artists and therefore too many artworks, and it is hard to make art *and* sell it (they are two very different, almost opposite professions), thirdly, many artists are wary of the so-called glamour and the flakiness of advertisement and the influencer, fourthly, non-artists think that art should be given away to them or offered at very low prices when the artist is not very well-known.

The latter baffles me every time. I have quite a stack of drawings under my bed, and it is eyed eagerly by a couple of lawyers, doctors, and a psychologist. They all earn tenfold what I make, but they want it free of charge. I often give away my work, but not to those who expect it. I produce a lot: writings, drawings, and paintings. I don't believe in "inspiration." My well never dries up. I want to have written a hundred books before I die, and I don't give a damn about the critics. I will always paint. Even when my hand does not want to hold the brush anymore, I will persevere, like Chris Tate, the painter who is described elsewhere in this bundle. Both Chris Tate and I are utterly unfamous and would like to keep it that way.

Looking here, looking there

"In the beginners' mind there are many possibilities; in the expert mind, there are few". Shunryu Suzuki Roshi.

This is about using seeing, just simple seeing with the eyes into the world, for waking up to the true nature of reality; about not seeing only half of reality but the whole of it. This seeing is, in fact, known by many names: enlightenment, awakening, nirvana, self-realization, self-transcendence, satori, samadhi… I prefer the simple name seeing. Seeing is knowing (seeing) without a doubt who/what we are. There is a bit of a taboo on seeing who we really are. Alan Watts calls this "our tacit conspiracy to ignore what or who we really are." As we all know, seeing is not difficult; on the contrary, it is the easiest thing. It does not take time. I can do it now, here. I must do it now, here; there is no other way. I am never not ready for seeing. What most don't know is that seeing is beneficial. The trouble with seeing is that it is hard to explain, but it can be shown in a simple way, I think, with the help of experiments that show seeing.

I look at my inward-pointing hand. It points at where I believe my face is. What is it pointing at?

I invite you to look at this pointing finger, your pointing finger. What is it pointing at exactly? You might say: "my face". But have you ever seen your face in the flesh? Are you sure it is there? Please, let me rattle this belief for just a little while… Seeing into the true nature of reality is like looking at the colour green (or any other colour for that matter). How to describe the experience of green or red, or blue? To See, I must do some experiments - really do them. Just thinking of them or imagining that you are doing them will not do the trick. Here comes the first experience of looking and seeing:

I point at an object that is about ten meters away from me. Let's say that lamp there. I mindfully take it in: colour: yellow, texture: paper, the being the thing it is: glowing, cozy… I note that it is out there, but also in here, where my head is supposed to be. It is so clearly here, in me, that I fleetingly become the lamp, so to speak.

I point at an object that is about three meters away from me, for example, that stray shoe there. Anything will do, but I chose the stray shoe. And I mindfully take it in: colour: blue, texture: cotton-ish, some other attributes it has: Modern; familiar. I note that it is out there, but also in here, where people tell me my head is. It is so clearly here, in my centre, that I fleetingly become the shoe.

I point at my own foot. How strange it is! I look at it as if I've never seen it before. Its color, shape, and texture - all unique and fascinating. I note that it is both out there and in here, where I believe my head to be. I scrutinize it objectively, as if I had to draw it. But am I in that foot? Do I know what it feels and smells like inside? No. Have I become the foot? Fleetingly, perhaps, as it replaced the lamp and the shoe in my vision. But I am not the foot, nor am I in it. So where am I? I point at my chest and wonder if this is where I reside. What is it like inside? Warm? Sticky? Crowded? Does it stink? No, I am not in there. I take a good look at it: its color, shape, texture, movements - all characteristics of a water creature, like a medium-sized seal, sleeping. I notice that it is both out there and in here, where I have been taught my head is. I look at it as if I had to draw it, forgetting everything I learned about a chest. It's a peculiar thing. And now, I turn my hand around 180 degrees and point to where my face should be. Like this:

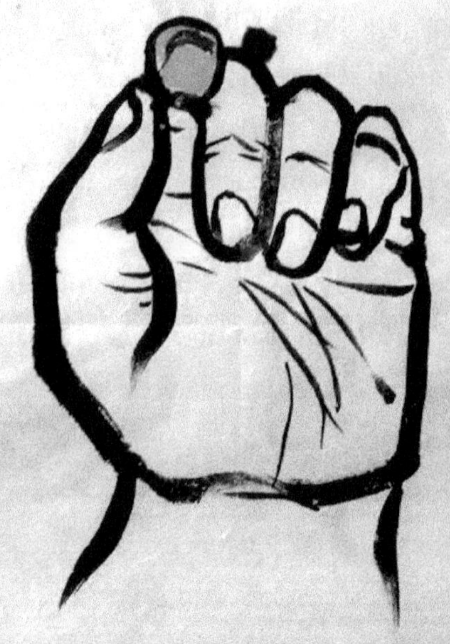
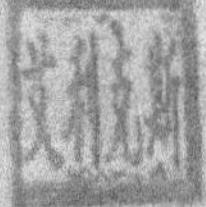

Just like before, I notice what I am pointing at, but this time the experience is diff erent. I notice that I am pointing at an open space, rather than a face. I forget everything I have learned about my face through other people, mirrors, photos, books...I look and clearly see that I am pointing at a void, a pure and empty capacity for the world. It's wonderfully strange.

I notice that all the things I have pointed at before - the lamp, the shoe, my foot, my chest - are not only out there, but also in here, in my center. There is no separation, no distance. This is incredibly mysterious. The lamp is there and the lamp is here simultaneously. I am looking in two directions at once - inwards and outwards - realizing and seeing that I am empty, pure capacity for the world, and at the same time, without any eff ort, the world, those things out there, are fi lling me to the brim. I realize that what I thought was my face is an illusion from my point of view. Or is it even that? I imagine it is there. Or is it even an imagination? I have made a mental map of my face and put it there. Yes, that's what it is - a map. Others may see my face, but I never will. My face, to me, exists only where I am not: in mirrors, in other people, in shiny surfaces like spoons and dead TV screens, and darkened windows. I might even keep it in a jar by the door.

I look around and see that my face is everywhere except where it is supposed to be. Look and see. Do you agree? Do you see?

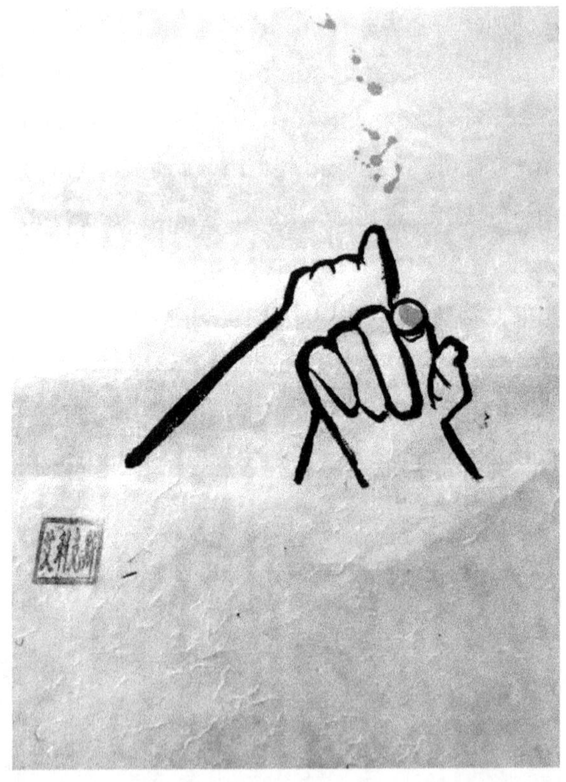

When the artist and the viewer disappear

Michelangelo once stated that he could already see the sculpture within the block of marble, even when it was still just a block. By creating empty spaces within the marble, the sculpture was revealed. "I see the angel and carve to set her free. It is easy, I carve to the skin and stop there," he remarked.

Paul Cèzanne would study a still-life for several hours before painting the empty spaces between objects, allowing the objects to emerge from the emptiness.

Many artists, especially great artists, describe the process of creating artwork as if they are not overly involved, as if the artwork created itself or was created by something or someone greater than the artist, working through them.

In true art, the artist is invisible. This is particularly evident in architecture. We do not continually desire to meet the architect of the house or building in which we reside or work. A skilled architect forces us to meet ourselves. It is incredibly dull to be presented with the architect's "interesting mind" every time we open a door due to the door handle's "fascinating" design. True talent is demonstrated when we do not have to think about the door handle at all. When we are reminded that the door handle is so intriguing, it becomes kitsch. When the door handle is designed well, we step through the door and meet ourselves.

Gaudí is an architect whom we are forced to meet constantly when we visit his buildings. The details of his monstrous cathedral in Barcelona scream: Look how interesting I am. Holy moley! Even after his passing, we are compelled to examine his mind. Forever.

Self-expression in art, the expression of emotions and feelings, often leads to the most dreadful kitsch. A good artist leaves me with myself, not with them. A sublime artist causes both the viewer and the creator to disappear. We both vanish into the artwork. For just a brief period, we become the artwork, providing a respite from the world.

Where drawing and language meet

Ode to Japan

I have adored, loved, and will always love Japan; the country I called home for eleven years, the country that best comprehends the concepts I have discussed in this book. No other place celebrates emptiness as extravagantly as Japan.

In *shodo*, the Japanese art of calligraphy, which I have studied for over thirty years) the white of the paper is as crucial as the black strokes brushed onto it. The Japanese visually play with words, giving the language an additional layer. A Japanese poem is not only a language experience but also a visual experience.

I have studied the art of painting plants and animals (*sumie*) for many years, never growing weary of it. A few suggestive brushstrokes are placed in a sea of white background for maximum impact.

Shodo is an art form that entails writing stylized characters using a brush and ink. In Japanese calligraphy, there are three primary styles known as *kaisho, gyosho*, and *sosho*.

Kaisho, which means "correct writing," is the most formal of the three styles. It is most commonly taught in schools and used in official documents and on formal occasions. In kaisho, each character is written with care and precision, with distinct, clean lines and regular spacing. It is a highly controlled and structured style that reflects the traditional values of discipline and respect.

Gyosho, which means "semi-cursive," is a more fluid and expressive style than kaisho. It is less formal and is often used in more casual settings, such as letters and notes. In gyosho, the characters are written more rapidly and spontaneously, with some lines and strokes connected to create a more flowing and graceful appearance. It is a more relaxed and personal style that allows writers to express their character and style.

Sosho, which means "cursive," is the most fluid and artistic of the three styles. It is the least formal and is often used in artistic compositions and calligraphy artworks. It is used by monks as an art form and mindfulness practice. In sosho, the characters are written with sweeping brushstrokes that flow together to create a dynamic, flowing composition. It is an expressive and personal style that allows writers to express their vision.

Noh Theatre incorporates silences and still poses that are so prolonged that most Westerners flee the theatre in horror.

Traditional Japanese music frequently features extended silences.

Ikebana, the art of flower arrangement, is a play

with form and no-form, with no-form winning.

In Japanese novels and films, nothing much happens.

Japanese poetry, particularly haiku, is extremely minimal. Here is an example from Basho:

Even in Kyoto
hearing the cuckoo's cry
I long for Kyoto

Japanese architecture (*Nihon kenchiku*) surpasses even the starkest minimalism in the West.

Martial arts are also about emptiness. *Karate* means "empty hand." The warrior must be empty to fight. His enemy will fill him with the strength he needs. He then employs that strength against the enemy. He borrows the enemy's strength.

Materials used in Japanese art are easily perishable: paper, wood, reed, water-based ink, flowers...

No other place understands impermanence as Japan does. The Japanese are masters of elimination and minimalism.

The concept of *muga*; no-self, is widely accepted. One is regarded as a part of the whole (of society and community), and the whole is always more important than the individual.

Self-expression is not encouraged and is frowned

upon, thus there are no traditional expressive art forms.

Mono-aware is deeply ingrained sentiment that every Japanese person is familiar with. It is similar to what Buddhists call *dukkha* and Michael Leuning calls "lifeache." It concerns the sadness of being human and the acceptance of that sadness.

Japan, of course, developed Zen, a philosophy rather than a religion, and the ultimate philosophy of emptiness and no-self.

Because of this all Japan rocks like no other place.

Movement

There is an extensive record throughout the centuries of how people have seen the world through paintings, drawings, photography, and film. A more recent addition is computer games.

Perspective in painting and drawing was discovered during the Renaissance in Europe, the time of the Enlightenment. Prior to perspective, paintings were constructed like flat screens that partially covered each other to create an illusion of depth. Color was used to suggest depth, with the landscape often painted blue in the background and colorful in the foreground. This created the illusion of depth.

The discovery of the mathematical principles of perspective made paintings more realistic. Perspective, however, is counter-intuitive; one must look very mindfully to see that it is "true" from an objective point of view. When one draws haphazardly what one thinks one is seeing, after a few minutes, it becomes apparent that the intended drawing looks like crap!

In the twentieth century, painters experimented with the idea that ignoring the rules of perspective produced a different reality.

With the invention of the camera, we no longer had to worry about observing, understanding, and measuring three-dimensional reality; we could simply trace a photographic image to get the perspective right. A lens is never deluded, so we learned to see reality with less delusion.

Film has given us an increasingly realistic view of reality. Recent developments in virtual reality have brought us a new perspective on moving reality: the subjective, first-person experience. Contemporary games are challenging our old-school conviction (delusion) that we are moving and the world is still. In many games, the world is seen from deep within the main character, similar to the drawing by Ernst Mach shown elsewhere in this bundle. We see part of the main character's body, just like in Mach's drawing, only now there is motion too. Arms, legs, feet, trees, houses, plants, birds, and knees are all moving in one soup of movement. Filming from this perspective makes things even more realistic, for example by taping a camera to the forehead.

Game shows us that from the deep, subjective first person perspective, we are completely still, and the world is moving. When we attach a camera to our forehead, or hold it in our mouth, or implant it in our nose and film while we're on a bicycle, walking, driving, or flying, we can see this. I kid you not: the world is moving, and I am not.

When I climb on my bike, I see the road racing

beneath me. When I drive my car, I see the landscape hurrying past. When I carefully observe, I notice that there are many layers in that landscape, and some move faster than others. Some layers move backward, other layers move forward.

When I take a plane, I see the earth moving.

When I take a walk, I push the ground away under my feet, as if I were walking on a giant ball. Wait, I am walking on a giant ball!

When I look at the world from my still center, what I see is ever-moving reality. This reality is visiting me, not the other way around.

I am not the one moving through the landscape, the cityscape, or the cloudscape; it is moving through me too.

When I book a trip, my destination comes to me. What a luxury.

Paper

The medium we draw on can be anything. As with so many things, expensive paper is often the best. However, other surfaces not meant for drawing can be very attractive as well. I studied law and found law books to be very expensive and quickly outdated. Hence, I use them as sketch paper. The result is often surprisingly beautiful. Old Bibles, novels, or books in other languages like Chinese, Japanese, or Arabic are also very useful, not to mention maps. These items can still be found in op shops, but they will gradually disappear with the disappearance of paper media.

I have used the same paper for forty years. It is a Japanese Washi of superior quality that I made during a silent retreat while staying in a Zen monastery in Japan. I lived with the nuns there for four months. The small monastery, temple, dojo, and workshop were all grouped on a low mountain in the forest.

After breakfast and morning meditation, we would go into the forest to cut saplings of the Gampi Tree, Misumata Shrub, and Mulberry bush. When we all had one hand full of sticks, we would return to the monastery and head to the workshop. We dumped the saplings into large concrete vessels filled with water from the nearby mountain stream to soak overnight.

We took a handful of soaked saplings from a day or so ago to a heavy wooden table to pound them into fiber with a wooden bat. When we washed the pulp in wooden buckets, the bark would float to the top and be removed. The clean pulp was dumped into a concrete vessel with clean water.

The roots of blue hibiscus plants had been soaking overnight in buckets and had produced a clear, glue-like substance. This was added to the wood fibers and mixed with a large wooden paddle. Now the substance was ready for scooping.

A fine bamboo net was stretched between the two halves of a wooden frame and lowered into the water that contained fiber and glue. One had to rock the frame smoothly between one's hands while lifting it out of the water to get an even layer of fiber on the bamboo, while the water fell back into the concrete vessel. The number of scoops determined the thickness of the paper. It took three scoops for a medium-thick sheet of Washi. The frames varied in size from A4 to A1.

The bamboo mat was freed from its frame and placed pulp-down onto a large slab of wood and was carefully peeled away from the pulp layer. The pulp layer was brushed onto the slab with a soft brush until there were no bubbles or other irregularities.

Every slab could hold four to six sheets. When the slabs were covered with pulp sheets on both sides, they were carried outside by two people and placed leaning against a tree. The pulp would be dry in half an hour to an hour, depending on the sun and the temperature. When dry, it only stuck lightly to the wood of the slab and could be easily peeled away from it. A brilliant sheet of paper with rugged edges was the result. When we left them too long and it was windy, the sheets of dry paper would fly around, and we had to retrieve them from trees and the moss on the ground.

The dry sheets were stacked in piles of ten. A paper ribbon was tied around each pile. The ribbon was made of hand-scooped paper in which flowers were embedded. The paper was sold in a small shop in the hallway of the monastery. People on retreat and those who worked in the workshop could purchase it at a discount.

The whole process, from the forest to the shop, took place in silence. The only sounds were the pounding of wood on wood, the streaming of water, and the wind in the trees.

After a few days of work, meditation, and eating two simple meals a day, the chatter in my head calmed down, and a pleasant routine from moment to moment was the result. I scooped paper for about 120 days.

I decided to buy a thousand A1 sheets and ship the extremely heavy pile to Tokyo, where I lived at the time. Initially, I used the paper for *shodo*, Japanese calligraphy. Then, when I moved back to Europe and later to Australia, I took the slowly dwindling pile with me. Now, forty years later, I still use it for my life drawing in Alice Springs. It is as luminous as after it was freshly scooped.

When other drawers recognise the quality of my paper and ask me where I bought it, I tell them this story.

Time Management

Time management is a constant struggle for most artists. All but a select few must juggle a job, household chores, children, social commitments, and their artistic pursuits. Only a handful of wealthy artists can afford to solely focus on their art.

People often question why I don't go out much. Even in Alice Springs, where there are plenty of art-related events, my preference is to create art. I spend a lot of time writing and drawing in my own space. There is simply not enough time in a lifetime to consume art and make it simultaneously. I enjoy being alone when I write; it's like traveling while staying at home. After a writing session, I often feel refreshed. Drawing is more challenging for me to start, so I prefer to be part of a drawing group.

Another reason why I don't go out much is that there was a time in my life when I consumed a lot of art. I lived in big cities like Amsterdam and Tokyo, where the quality of art was exceptional. I had subscriptions to the theatre, ballet, and opera, and frequented exhibitions of visual arts. In Alice Springs, I worked in Aboriginal Art galleries. I feel like I've consumed enough art for a lifetime. Therefore, "not going out much" is related to managing my time.

The reason why most artists in the past were men has a

lot to do with women being responsible for childcare. This too is a time management issue. Although there are now more female artists than male artists in Australia, women are still paid 30% less than their male counterparts.

There is a myth that artists are messy individuals. Compared to my friends who meticulously fold their clothes, I am rather untidy. I toss my clothes into a drawer straight from the clothesline without any Marie Kondo-like joy of folding or sorting by color. Why? Because it takes time. Time that I'd rather spend on my writing. I prepare the quickest recipes and find the most efficient ways to do chores that cannot be avoided, all to free up more time for my writing.

Ink

Not only did I make my own paper, but I also make my own inks. I prefer ink for drawing because it leaves no room for doubt. What's done is done, and one can't go back like with a pencil or charcoal and an eraser.

The medium one draws with should be of superior quality, yet there are tools that are cheap and effective, like bamboo pens. One can make them by sharpening a piece of bamboo with a Stanley knife. Although expensive Japanese brushes are great to have, a simple branch from a tree does a good job too, or a feather., or a toothbrush. It all depends what marks you are after.

In my opinion, the best ink for drawing is bistre. Bistre can refer to two things: a very dark shade of grayish-brown, or a shade of brown made from soot. Beechwood or walnut peel is burned to produce the soot, which is then boiled and diluted with water. Many Old Masters used bistre as the ink for their drawings. The first recorded use of bistre as a color name in English was in 1727. Another name for the color bistre is soot brown.

I use walnut peel for my inks, burning it in a small oven until it is black. I pound it into a powder and boil it in water until the water has evaporated. I then dilute the resulting powder with water when needed. It is easier to store the powder than the liquid ink, so I make a batch whenever I need one.

Most bistre is a sepia color. The exact color resulting from the burning process depends on the temperature and the amount of oxygen during the process. Sometimes the soot produces red sepia or a yellow, occasionally even blue or green.

The ink has little body, so it can be used as a wash to suggest shadows. By adding a little Indian ink to the mix, one can achieve a good line drawing ink.

Making ink is extremely messy and should ideally be done outside wearing old clothes that can be disposed of afterwards because the soot easily spreads to other objects on touches.

Bistre can be bought in small bottles, with 30 ml typically costing around $15.